Lessons in Writing

By

R.E. MYERS

COPYRIGHT © 2005 Mark Twain Media, Inc.

ISBN 1-58037-308-9

Printing No. CD-404035

Mark Twain Media, Inc., Publishers
Distributed by Carson-Dellosa Publishing Company, Inc.

Table of Contents

Introduction

My approach to writing this book has been to present a variety of writing forms in a palatable manner. The lessons are meant to be engaged in by intermediate students, but many are suitable for both older and younger students. The philosophy undergirding the lessons coincides roughly with the prevailing methodological notions concerning pre-writing (conception), incubation, production, and revision. Pre-writing is given full emphasis because my own orientation is based on the creative thinking principles of E. Paul Torrance (1990, 1999), and I believe that the warm-up is crucial to all creative production. The goal of *Lessons in Writing,* then, is to increase the writing skills of middle-grade students in an enjoyable way.

The sequence of the lessons has a pattern, but it's not necessary to administer them in numerical order. Perhaps your students have had several lessons dealing with similes or alliteration; in that case, you can choose to give only one or none of those lessons offered here. Similarly, you might decide to administer one type of writing before another, thus changing the order of the lessons. In all candor, I do hope you alter both the order of the lessons and their content according to the abilities and experiences of your students. You should feel that you are a full-fledged co-author of this publication.

References:

Torrance, E.P. and H.T. Safter. *The Incubation Model of Teaching.* Buffalo, NY: Bearly Limited, 1990.

Torrance, E.P. and H.T. Safter. *Making the Creative Leap Beyond.* Buffalo, NY: Creative Education Foundation Press, 1999.

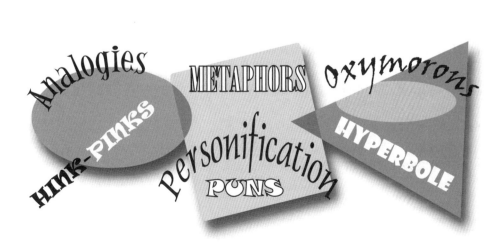

Lesson 1: Similes

What's It Like?: Producing Eleven Original Similes; Predicting How People Will Live in 100 Years

TO THE TEACHER/PARENT: ABOUT THE LESSON

This lesson was designed to make students aware of the richness and also the drabness of our speech. The initiating activity offers you an opportunity to point out to your students how imitative and unresourceful we can be in our speech patterns.

The idea the student is invited to analyze at the second level is that the human mind constantly makes comparisons. Some of your students may have trouble in understanding the importance of this ability, so you should be prepared to give examples of its significance.

A number of students of the creative thinking process regard the ability to see relationships as the very essence of the process. Long ago, Spearman (1930) stated this as his second principle in explaining "mental creativity." "When two or more items (precepts or ideas) are given, a person may perceive them to be in various ways related; thus, one may be near, after, or the cause of, or a part of the other" (p. 18). In their classic study of highly creative adolescents, Getzels and Jackson (1960) concluded that the very essence of their subjects' creativity lay in their ability to produce new ideas by joining together things that are customarily thought of as independent and dissimilar to go off in new directions.

If the student accepts the invitation to compare living today with what he or she envisions it to be like in the next century, the student will be using both his imaginative and critical faculties to a considerable extent. The student will therefore be emulating the scientist, who in searching for new knowledge continually pushes beyond what is known and then evaluates what has been learned by using measures that experience has taught can be trusted.

EVALUATING STUDENT RESPONSES

Answers for the similes will vary. Accept all reasonable answers.

Targeted Learner Outcomes: The student will

- complete ten similes by supplying words other than the all-too-familiar ones,

- think up a simile about a dinosaur, and

- predict major changes in how people will live 100 years from now.

Lesson 1: Similes

What's It Like?: Producing Eleven Original Similes; Predicting How People Will Live in 100 Years (cont.)

FOLLOWING THROUGH

If your students become especially interested in colorful language, ask them to compile lists of the picturesque expressions they run across in their reading. You can supply some favorites of your own to get things rolling. As you probably know, *Reader's Digest* has a feature called "Picturesque Patter" that is a rich source of quaint sayings.

References:

Getzels, J.W. and P.W. Jackson. The Study of Giftedness: A Multidimensional Approach. In *The Gifted Student.* Washington, D.C.: Government Printing Office, 1960.

Spearman, C. *Creative Mind.* London: Cambridge University Press, 1930.

"Sharp as a tack"

"Snug as a bug in a rug"

3

Name: _____ Date: _____

Lesson 1: Similes

What's It Like?

A. Do you know what similes are? **Similes point out likenesses or similarities in things.** Have you ever heard expressions such as "sharp as a tack" or "snug as a bug in a rug"? When we talk like that, we are using similes. You will usually find the word *as* or the word *like* in a simile because these are the connecting words we use to make comparisons.

Directions: The idea of this exercise is to have you think of similes that are unusual and colorful. In each item below, some part of a simile is given. Your job is to make a comparison, using the words given and some other words. Fill in as many blanks as you can. If you can't think of an appropriate word or phrase, go on to the next item. You can come back to the one you were "stuck on" later when an idea comes to you. Try to be original in your comparisons.

1. scarce as _____

2. like finding _____

3. funny as _____

4. hard as _____

5. crooked as _____

6. wet as _____

7. soft as _____

8. like mixing _____

9. sells like _____

10. nervous as _____

11. Now, let's reverse the process. Can you think of an adjective that fits a dinosaur?

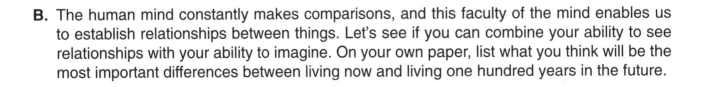

_____

B. The human mind constantly makes comparisons, and this faculty of the mind enables us to establish relationships between things. Let's see if you can combine your ability to see relationships with your ability to imagine. On your own paper, list what you think will be the most important differences between living now and living one hundred years in the future.

Lesson 2: Metaphors

Losing Heads: Writing a Conversation With Metaphors

TO THE TEACHER/PARENT: ABOUT THE LESSON

<u>**First Level**</u>: **Sketching misconceptions that small children might have**

Most of your students will be able to recognize in themselves the small children that are referred to by us when we discuss the misconceptions that little ones have when they hear many figures of speech. The tremendous joy that they derive from their progress in understanding adults is mitigated at times by the confusion that comes from an expression such as "He lost his head" (hence our title, "Losing Heads"). To be truthful, children aren't the only ones who take these metaphors literally. Depending upon our frame of mind and the kind of language used, any of us can be confused by a metaphor that somehow throws us off the speaker's track.

We have presented sentences that your students are to interpret as a young child might, but the interpretations are to be sketched rather than written. There are a couple of reasons for asking your students to draw rather than write their responses. First of all, we intend to provide a little relief from the direct approach of requiring written responses to the queries in this book. Secondly, there are many young people who enjoy drawing, and this will give the students who do well in nonverbal expression an opportunity to exhibit their talents.

<u>**Second Level**</u>: **Listening for metaphors**

Although we define metaphor in the lesson, you may want to elaborate upon our definition. It's a tricky figure of speech to pin down without illustrations, and so additional examples of very common metaphors will help those who confuse metaphors with other figures of speech. The best examples, of course, are those that are used by the students themselves.

Your students are to listen for metaphors during a 24-hour period. This will provide you a natural break in the lesson, which we feel will work to your advantage inasmuch as it will permit a good deal of reinforcement of the concept and also stretch out a lesson that really needs time to take hold and develop in the student's mind.

<u>**Third Level**</u>: **Incorporating metaphors into written conversation**

Stories benefit greatly when the writer uses conversation; plays are nothing without it, and even student reports are enhanced by quotations from interviewees. Thus, much is to be gained by the student in being able to capture natural conversation in writing. A case could be made, then, for introducing this lesson early in the school year because increased skill in handling conversation in a story or report will improve much of your students' writing. The difficulty in making the conversation natural can be overcome in part by attending to the way people express themselves in words. This lesson will give you an opportunity to train the ears of your students in catching the rhythm and flavor of conversation.

Name: _____ Date: _____

Lesson 2: Metaphors

Losing Heads

A. Young children sometimes take what we say quite literally—and it confuses them. They are confused by how we express ourselves in figurative language, as when someone says: "You can't blame Sam for biting his head off—Dan was way out of line." A child hearing this might well have a vision of a decapitated boy and could also wonder why Dan got out of the line, especially if he could be bitten so brutally for it. And when a young child hears something like "With all the confusion, he lost his head and ran the wrong way," he or she might have a similar vision.

Directions: Imagine what a confused child would visualize when he or she hears the following expressions. In the space below, draw a sketch of one of the scenes that might come to the child's mind.

1. Mr. Thomas was a rock throughout the crisis.

2. After Sean's nasty remark, Terry stared a hole through him.

3. Justin scorched the road to Junction City in his convertible because he was in such a hurry to get there.

4. Before long, the detective was able to sniff out the clue that solved the case.

5. The bad news hit him in the face.

6. Unfortunately, Robert just wallowed in self-pity after she turned him down.

7. Rita was all puffed up because she had won the prize.

Name: _____ Date: _____

Lesson 2: Metaphors

Losing Heads (cont.)

B. It's not uncommon to hear expressions such as those we've given; you hear them all the time. You can probably hear dozens if you listen carefully during the next 24 hours. Try to remember at least four and write them in the space below. This kind of expression is called a **metaphor. It occurs when words that are generally used in one field of experience are used in another,** such as in the expression, "Don't make a pig of yourself." You understand what "making a pig of yourself" means, but if you took the saying literally, it would be telling you not to change yourself into an animal (if you did have the magic power to do so).

SOME METAPHORS I'VE HEARD:

1. _____

2. _____

3. _____

4. _____

C. During the past 24 hours, you've probably heard a few of the most common metaphors in our language, and you may have heard one or two that were unusual. Some expressions are found only in a particular part of the country, and they sound strange when a native of that region says them outside his or her area. Why don't you write a conversation between two people that has at least two metaphors in it? The conversation can be one you heard or one you made up yourself.

_____

_____

_____

_____

_____

_____

Lesson 3: Alliteration

Shabby Shoes: Producing Alliterative Phrases; Composing Couplets

TO THE TEACHER/PARENT: ABOUT THE LESSON

The exercise at the beginning of the lesson that has students producing alliterative modifiers for the 24 articles of clothing leads in to the writing activity of composing couplets. Inasmuch as couplets are quite brief, the task shouldn't daunt your students. In addition, couplets are easy to write because of the rhyming. For those who get stuck in thinking of alliterative adjectives, it will be quite all right to allow them to use a dictionary, since the idea is just to get your students to produce alliterative phrases.

EVALUATING STUDENT RESPONSES

As long as the responses are in good taste, you need only note which students are fluent in producing alliterations. Some possible responses to the prompts are given below.

shoes: shabby, shiny, sensible, stout, sturdy, sharp, simple, soft

scarf: scratchy, shear, sharp, scrumptious

belt: boy's, brown, black, blue

jacket: jumbled, jeweled

blouse: brown, blue, beaded, bleached, brocade

boots: black, brown, beat-up, boxy, burnished, beautiful

stockings: stunning, Sunday, shear, stippled, sticky, silk

sandals: slippery, scandalous, stupid, sensible, strappy

hat: handsome, horrible, hard

sweater: sweet, sharp, spring, standard, sleeveless, sweltering, soft

cap: creepy, comfortable, curious

socks: slippery, sloppy, smelly

trousers: tight, tattered, tan

pants: pin-striped, pleated, purple, pink, pressed

muffler: moth-eaten, mauve, musty, maroon

headband: heavy, homemade, handsome

coat: camel's-hair, casual, comfortable

vest: velvet, versatile, vermilion, vile

serape: simple, cerise, silver, splendid

skirt: sensible, skimpy, summer, simple, shiny, scandalous, smooth

collar: crisp, cutting, curious, crimson

cuffs: classy, clean, crisp

shirt: stuffed, striped, starched, short, sanitized, sensible, summer, sleeveless, short-sleeved

tie: tan, terrific, terrible, tasteful, tasteless

Targeted Learner Objectives: The student will

- produce alliterative phrases for 24 articles of clothing.

- write at least two couplets that incorporate alliteration.

Name: _____ Date: _____

Lesson 3: Alliteration

Shabby Shoes

A. You have probably heard of "knobby knees" and "chubby cheeks," and you may have even heard of a "furrowed forehead." Those expressions are examples of the use of **alliteration. It's the common device of using words with the same initial sounds next to or near each other.**

Directions: See if you can come up with alliterative couplings for these clothing items.

1. shoes _____
2. scarf _____
3. belt _____
4. jacket _____
5. blouse _____
6. boots _____
7. stockings _____
8. sandals _____

9. hat _____
10. sweater _____
11. cap _____
12. socks _____
13. trousers _____
14. pants _____
15. muffler _____
16. headband _____

17. coat _____
18. vest _____
19. serape _____
20. skirt _____
21. collar _____
22. cuffs _____
23. shirt _____
24. tie _____

B. If you have chosen an adjective such as shabby or shiny to go with shoes, you might have the beginning of a couplet like this one:

> Sloppy Sal's shabby shoes
> Gave all her fancy friends the blues.

Then you might add another of the alliterative expressions and come up with:

> Sloppy Sal's shabby shoes
> Gave all her fancy friends the blues;
> But when she wore her beat-up boots,
> They filled the air with nasty hoots.

Directions: See if you can produce two couplets that incorporate some of the alliterative expressions you've written for the clothing items. Write the couplets on your own paper.

Lesson 4: Alliteration

Blending: Finding Synonyms for Alliterative Consonant Blends; Writing Sentences With Alliterative Consonant Blends; Writing a Short Story

TO THE TEACHER/PARENT: ABOUT THE LESSON

"Blending" has several aspects. Superficially it is about alliteration, but not too much is made of that device in the lesson. It also has the student producing consonant blends. Your students have been exposed to many exercises dealing with consonant blends, and so they should be thoroughly familiar with the task of pronouncing and writing words that start with *pr, cl, st, gr,* and *pl.*

In a real sense, "Blending" is concerned with developing the student's vocabulary. By asking for words that are similar, we're causing the student to go beyond popping out words with the same initial sound and to search for words that meet the requirement of being alike. For example, if you were asked to produce words that start with *cr,* you might come up with *crop, crib, crab, crabby, crust, crumb, cry, cringe, cross, crawl, crunch, crumple,* and *cryptic* fairly quickly. Which of them could be picked out as being alike? Maybe *crunch* and *crumple,* but surely *crabby* and *cross.*

Another element in the vocabulary aspect of this lesson is that the student is looking for synonyms (although that term doesn't appear in the lesson). As you can see, you can use "Blending" to stress more than one language skill. But more importantly, this lesson can be used as a story starter. The story starters are the sentences the students generate at the third level.

First Level: Producing words that have the same consonant blends and finding two that are similar

Five consonant blends are listed at the beginning of the lesson, and the first task for the student is to write down a number of words that start with those consonant blends. After producing the words, the student is asked to circle two that are similar (have similar meanings). If you give this part of the lesson to your class orally, you may find that all of your students have not gotten their consonant blends right. You may also discover that, in circling the two words that are similar, words have been paired that are not enough alike. Our ploy is that the student will have to do some thinking in order to find two words that are really similar. You will want to proceed as slowly with this initiating activity as seems prudent. With practice, your students will be writing words with the same beginning sounds and matching similar words with some degree of proficiency.

Second Level: Writing sentences that contain the matched pairs of words

Carrying the game a little further, we ask for a sentence from each of the lines of consonant blends. Again, the student must do a little thinking to produce the sentences. That is what we are after.

Lesson 4: Alliteration

Blending: Finding Synonyms for Alliterative Consonant Blends; Writing Sentences With Alliterative Consonant Blends; Writing a Short Story (cont.)

Third Level: Writing stories inspired by the students' responses

The culminating phase of the lesson has your students writing a story based on one of the sentences produced at the second level. The spark of a good plot may be struck in the writing of one of those sentences, or the sentences could all be pedestrian and dull. However, we hope that some will prove to be effective story starters. A few tips are given at the end to remind your students to supply enough details in order to make their stories interesting. You may want to supplement what we have said.

EVALUATING STUDENT RESPONSES

These are acceptable synonyms for the consonant blends:

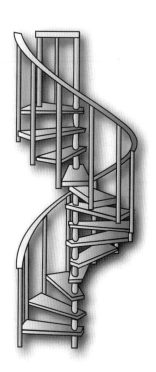

    pr   predict and prognosticate

    cl   clump and cluster (possibly clear and clean)

    st   stair and step

    gr   great and grand (possibly grip and grapple)

    pl   plate and platter

Targeted Learner Outcomes: The student will

- understand how alliteration is used,

- recognize and use consonant blends,

- provide synonyms for five consonant blends,

- write five sentences containing consonant blends, and

- write a short story inspired by one of the five sentences.

Name: _____ Date: _____

Lesson 4: Alliteration

Blending

A. There are many games about words that have the same sounds, but most of them are about rhyme. Instead of the endings being alike, in this game, the beginnings are alike. In the nursery rhyme, "Sing a song of sixpence," we have an example of **alliteration, where the initial sound of words in a phrase is repeated.** We can also have alliteration with consonant blends. An example is the line a songwriter wrote, "Who knows where or when?" The words *where* and *when* have the same beginning sound.

Directions: Write six or more words that come to your mind that start with each of these consonant blends.

1. *pr* _____

2. *cl* _____

3. *st* _____

4. *gr* _____

5. *pl* _____

Now go back and find two *pr* words that are alike in meaning. If you don't have two that are alike, try to think of another that will be like one of the words you wrote. Circle the two words that are similar in meaning. For example, if you were thinking of words that start with *bl,* you might write:

> black, blue, blunder, blank, bluster, blame, blunt, blare, blister, blast, bloom, bloke, blossom, blink.

The two words that are similar in this list are *bloom* and *blossom.* Circle those two words. Now circle the two words that are alike for each of the blends above.

B. Now write sentences with the two words you've chosen as being similar for each of the blends. For instance, using words with the *st* blend, you might think of a sentence such as "As Nancy was about to take a *step* toward the *stair,* she noticed how still the house had become." Write just one sentence for each of your lines.

1. *pr* _____

2. *cl* _____

Lesson 4: Alliteration

Blending (cont.)

3. *st* _____

4. *gr* _____

5. *pl* _____

C. In the sentence given on the previous page about the girl in the still house, what might happen next? Does the sentence make you slightly uneasy? If any of your own sentences get you to thinking, you might invent a plot and write a story. You can use the space below for making an outline of the plot.

_____

_____

_____

_____

_____

_____

_____

_____

_____

_____

After you have made an outline of your plot, think about the characters in your story. What are their special qualities? Be sure to describe them so that your readers can picture them in their minds. Then think about the setting for your story. Early in the story, you should describe the place where the action takes place so your readers can visualize the setting. Plan your story so it builds to a climax and has a satisfactory ending.

Lesson 5: Rhyme

Hink-Pinks: Producing Rhymed Pairs of Words

TO THE TEACHER/PARENT: ABOUT THE LESSON

The game of hink-pink (or hinky-pinky for words with two syllables) is well known through-out the land. Its continuing popularity is perhaps due to the fact that a seemingly inexhaustible number of rhyming words can be used in the game to stimulate the minds of young and old. Hink-pink is primarily included in this book because of the fascination young people have for rhyme.

Our only contribution to the game is to introduce the idea that by adding a rhyme, you can tell a story. You might encourage your students to play this variation of the game, which is more challenging than the original.

EVALUATING STUDENT RESPONSES

These are the intended hink-pinks for the 12 phrases, but others might work as well or better.

1. irritable supervisor = cross boss

2. angry boy = mad lad

3. eager adolescent = keen teen

4. blond twosome = fair pair

5. genuine transaction = real deal

6. tan dress = brown gown

7. small scare = slight fright

8. tidy chair = neat seat

9. principal hurt = main pain

10. benevolent intellect = kind mind

11. little row = small brawl

12. uninteresting seabird = dull gull

Targeted Learner Outcomes: The student will

- produce rhymed pairs of one-syllable words for the 12 definitions given, and

- think up an original hink-pink.

Name: _____ Date: _____

Lesson 5: Rhyme

Hink-Pinks

A. A **hink-pink is a rhyming pair of one-syllable words that is defined by a given phrase.** To form a hink-pink, study the clue phrase and think of two rhyming words that are synonyms for the words in the phrase. For example, an "unhappy pappy" could be called a "sad dad."

Directions: See if you can come up with a pair of rhyming words that is equivalent to each of the dozen phrases given below.

1. irritable supervisor _____

2. angry boy _____

3. eager adolescent _____

4. blond twosome _____

5. genuine transaction _____

6. tan dress _____

7. small scare _____

8. tidy chair _____

9. principal hurt _____

10. benevolent intellect _____

11. little row _____

12. uninteresting seabird _____

B. Can you think of another set of words in which one rhymed pair is nearly equal to another rhymed pair (for example, soggy doggy = wet pet)?

_____

Lesson 6: Rhyme

Hinky-Pinkies: Producing Pairs of Rhymed Words

TO THE TEACHER/PARENT: ABOUT THE LESSON

Hinky-pinkies are as popular as hink-pinks, being nearly as easy to devise. (There is also a three-syllable hinkety-pinkety, but we don't present that variation in this book.) The rhyming called for in this lesson is comparatively difficult; some of the prompts will probably cause a little head-scratching. However, hinky-pinkies are more for having fun than making a lot of sense.

EVALUATING STUDENT RESPONSES

These are the two-syllable rhyming words that are equivalent to the definitions given in the lesson, however other answers may also work.

1. stylish girl = classy lassie

2. amusing rabbit = funny bunny

3. noisy eating = crunching munching

4. lawful raptor = legal eagle

5. cheery gossip = cheerful earful

6. exceptionally cautious = very wary

7. cows' fight = cattle battle

8. cool flick = groovy movie

9. staggering sensation = reeling feeling

10. loving couple = woosome twosome

11. competent fur-bearer = able sable

12. indolent flower = lazy daisy

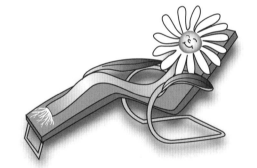

There are a number of two-syllable rhyming words that begin with "h" in the English language. Among them are helter-skelter, hurly-burly, hoity-toity, hanky-panky, hurdy-gurdy, and harum-scarum.

Targeted Learning Outcomes: The student will

• produce rhymed pairs of two-syllable words for the 12 definitions given, and

• produce at least three examples of hyphenated hinky-pinkies that start with the letter "h."

Name: _____ Date: _____

Lesson 6: Rhyme

Hinky-Pinkies

A. A **hinky-pinky is a pair of two-syllable rhyming words that is defined by a given phrase.**
To form a hinky-pinky, study the clue phrase and think of two rhyming words that are synonyms for the words in the phrase. For example, a "joyous father" is a "happy pappy."

Directions: Use a dictionary, if necessary, to come up with hinky-pinkies for these dozen
phrases.

1. stylish girl _____

2. amusing rabbit _____

3. noisy eating _____

4. astute lawyer _____

5. cheery gossip _____

6. exceptionally cautious _____

7. cows' fight _____

8. cool flick _____

9. staggering sensation _____

10. loving couple _____

11. competent fur-bearer _____

12. indolent flower _____

B. We have quite a few two-syllable hyphenated rhyming words in the English language.
"Fuddy-duddy," a person who is fussy and old-fashioned in his ways, is an example.

Directions: See if you can come up with three hyphenated two-syllable rhyming words that
start with the letter "h."

1. _____

2. _____

3. _____

Lesson 7: Puns

Punny Riddles: Solving Twelve Riddles; Composing Original Riddles

TO THE TEACHER/PARENT: ABOUT THE LESSON

The riddles in this lesson are puns, and for the most part, they are quite easy. Your students may race through them. The challenge, however, comes in the second part, where they must compose five or more original riddles that are based on puns. We believe that this task is not beyond their abilities because youngsters have been contributing riddles to *Highlights for Children* and other publications for decades.

EVALUATING STUDENT RESPONSES

These are the answers to the riddles.

1. When it is reddy/ready.
2. He didn't knead/need it.
3. In the barn next to Pa's cow.
4. Retire.
5. For his Punch 'n Judy.
6. A goat goes around abuttin'.
7. "Oh dear/deer!"
8. A lighthouse.
9. With 22 carrots/carats and a lot of bullion.
10. He'd gotten a birdie.
11. An airplane.
12. When you do it right, you get an abadile. When you do it wrong, you get a crocobalone.

Targeted Learner Outcomes: The student will

- solve 12 riddles, and

- compose at least five riddles that are based on puns.

Name: _____ Date: _____

Lesson 7: Puns

Punny Riddles

A. When you were younger, you probably heard the old riddle about when a door isn't a door (when it's ajar). That kind of riddle depends for its humor upon **a play on words—a pun.** All riddles don't have puns, but a great many do.

Directions: Here are some punny riddles that you may enjoy solving.

1. When is the best time to pick a tomato? _____

   _____

2. Why did the baker throw the extra dough away? _____

   _____

3. Where is Moscow? _____

   _____

4. What should a driver do when he has a second flat tire at night? _____

   _____

5. Why was the puppeteer arrested after his performance? _____

   _____

6. What goes around a button? _____

   _____

7. What did the gardener say when she saw the leafless rosebush and hoof prints near it?

   _____

8. What house weighs the least? _____

   _____

9. How do you make gold soup? _____

   _____

Name: _____ Date: _____

Lesson 7: Puns

Punny Riddles (cont.)

10. Why did the golfer crow after he fired his last shot?

    _____

11. If two wrongs don't make a right, what do two rights make?

    _____

12. What do you get when you cross an abalone and a crocodile?

    _____

    _____

B. Why don't you try your hand at thinking up riddles? In the space below, write at least five riddles that are based on puns.

_____

_____

_____

_____

_____

_____

_____

_____

_____

_____

Lesson 8: Puns

Brieflies: Devising Questions That Require Punny Answers

TO THE TEACHER/PARENT: ABOUT THE LESSON

In preparing for the lesson, you can give your students any word game—anagrams, acrostics, jumbles, or the like—and get them into the mood for this lesson. "Brieflies" use adverbs or adverbial phrases and rely on puns for their humor.

EVALUATING STUDENT RESPONSES

The answers to the 14 questions are as follows.

1. Highly
2. Barely
3. Earnestly
4. Honestly!
5. Ably
6. Hopelessly
7. Haltingly

8. Quietly
9. Amazingly well
10. Unfairly
11. Tastefully
12. Forcefully
13. Tempestuously
14. Fabulously well

The strategy we employ in writing a briefly is to find a likely adverb and then construct a question that can be answered by that word. The "story" derives from the question.

Targeted Learner Outcomes: The student will

• answer 14 questions with adverbs or adverbial phrases, and

• devise at least three questions that require punny answers and that are adverbs or adverbial phrases.

FOLLOWING THROUGH

Have students present their puns to one another orally or in writing. When written, they are usually easier to solve.

Name: _____ Date: _____

Lesson 8: Puns

Brieflies

A. Sometimes all you need in order to respond to a question is one or two words. The usual answers are "Yes" and "No," but in some cases you can use only one or two other words to adequately express your response. For example, let's say that Vincent, wearing only his undershorts, strolled from the bedroom into the kitchen, where he was surprised to find his wife with two women friends. How did Vincent present himself? A good answer that is also a pun would be "briefly!"

Directions: Let's see how good you are at coming up with short answers to questions such as the one above. What would you say in these situations? Make each answer an adverb and also a pun.

1. Doug is seven feet tall. He is an honest, hard-working electrician who often replaces light bulbs in ceilings without a ladder.

    How do you regard Doug? _____

2. Roger joined about a hundred swimmers in a race across the channel, but halfway across, he lost his trunks.

    How did he finish? _____

3. Ernest was a sincere, hard-working boy, but he was always hungry. One sunny Saturday his mother promised to bake a pie if Ernest would wash the car.

    Later on, when the mother saw her son outside, how was he tackling the job?

    _____

4. Jenny always tried to be the first one to finish the math tests. She studied very hard for them. A conscientious, sincere kind of girl, Jenny was shocked when a classmate asked her how she managed to finish so quickly—did she cheat?

    How did Jenny reply? _____

5. Of the three boys in his family, Abel was the youngest and brightest. His older brothers were klutzy when it came to fixing anything. When no one in the family could fix the broken screen door, Abel said he'd fix it.

    How did he handle the job? _____

Name: _____ Date: _____

Lesson 8: Puns

Brieflies (cont.)

6. Hope is the star player on her school's basketball team. Unfortunately for Hope and every member of the team, she broke her ankle diving for a ball during their last game.

   How do her teammates look at their next game against the leading team in the conference?

   _____

7. Private Wilson was shy and unsure of himself. He rarely spoke right out. One dark night, he came back to camp after a week's furlough and was stopped sharply by the sentry on duty.

   How did Private Wilson respond to the sentry? _____

8. On her birthday, Maria had a cold and lost her voice.

   How did she enjoy her birthday party? _____

9. On her first try, Vera went through the garden maze without a mistake.

   How did Vera do? _____

10. Tom hit a fly ball that was just barely foul, but the umpire ruled it fair, and so Tom had a homer that won the game. The umpire was Tom's uncle.

    How did the umpire behave? _____

11. Thelma served delicious luncheons with just the right table decorations.

    How did Thelma prepare her luncheons? _____

12. Kirk had a very strong personality, and he usually plunged right into a task with little fore-thought. When he couldn't work the combination of his lock so it would open, he pried it off with a crowbar.

    How did Kirk react to the problem with the lock? _____

13. Grant had a poor disposition, and he didn't like bad weather. When there was thunder and lightning for two days and winds reached 90 miles an hour, Grant ranted and raved at the violent storm.

    How did Grant react to the terrible weather? _____

Name: _____ Date: _____

Lesson 8: Puns

Brieflies (cont.)

14. Mr. Fendall likes to tell stories, and some of his favorites are the old fables. He is enormously successful when he tells the fables to little kids, delighting them every time.

   How well does Mr. Fendall tell stories to children? _____

B. See if you can come up with some questions with similar one- or two-word answers. Write at least three in the space below.

_____

_____

_____

_____

_____

_____

C. Now try your questions out on some friends. You will see how successful you were at composing punny questions. What method did you use in composing your questions?

_____

_____

_____

_____

Did it always work? _____

_____

_____

Lesson 9: Personification

Anthropomorphizing: Putting Personification in Weathergrams

TO THE TEACHER/PARENT: ABOUT THE LESSON

Personification is inherent in the thinking of human beings, and so it occurs naturally in our speech and writing. Some writers make great use of the device, but others do not employ it much at all. When used skillfully, personification is quite effective.

In this lesson, there is a good deal of discussion of personification before the student is asked to incorporate it into verse. The verse is the weathergram, an invention of Lloyd Reynolds (1902–1978) that is not widely known. Reynolds was inspired by the Shinto prayers written on slips of paper that are hung from trees in Japan. He and his students at Reed College in Portland, Oregon, hung their weathergrams from trees and shrubs on campus. The guidelines for writing a weathergram are given in the lesson.

Targeted Learner Outcomes: The student will

• gain an understanding of and appreciation for the use of personification in writing, and

• learn to write a weathergram.

FOLLOWING THROUGH

If your students enjoy writing weathergrams, you can encourage them to write more without concerning themselves with incorporating personification in the verses.

Reference:

Reynolds, L.J. *Weathergrams.* Portland, OR: Society for Italic Handwriting, Reed College, 1972.

Name: _____ Date: _____

Lesson 9: Personification

Anthropomorphizing

A. One of the favorite devices of many poets and novelists is personification. **Personification is a figure of speech in which a thing, quality, or idea is represented as a person.** This is also known as **anthropomorphizing—giving inanimate objects human characteristics.** These are some examples of how a novelist used personification to describe various scenes.

> "Locked within the great arms of the mountains, the water lay quiet as a burnished shield."

> "Water lapped softly under the bows and whispered along her sides."

> "The hill crowded in and cradled the water into a deep and narrow basin."

> "Shadows surged up towards me, pouncing from the corners of the dim lounge."

> "The enormous shadow of the mountain strode across the little valley."

B. Emily Dickinson was quite fond of using personification in her poems. This is a typical example.

The Past is such a curious creature
To look her in the Face
A transport may receipt us
Or a disgrace—

Unarmed if any meet her
I charge him fly
Her faded Ammunition
Might yet reply.

Sometimes we can effectively communicate an idea by means of personification, as Emily Dickinson did in the poem above. By making the Past a female person, the poet put over the idea that one's past can suddenly loom up to hurt someone.

Name: _____ Date: _____

Lesson 9: Personification

Anthropomorphizing (cont.)

C. Personification even works well with briefer poems such as the weathergram. This weathergram uses it in a conventional way.

> Wolf
> A wail—
>   in harmony
> with the freezing
>   breath of
>   winter

A weathergram has these characteristics:

1. It is about nature and the weather.

2. It is comprised of only a sentence or a sentence fragment and is usually 10–12 words long.

3. The emphasis is upon observing and reacting to nature.

4. It is primarily visual; words are arranged on the lines for dramatic effect.

5. Titles are optional.

Directions: Try composing at least two weathergrams based on a personification. You can choose a personification given on these pages or select one of your own.

_____

_____

_____

_____

_____

_____

Lesson 10: Personification

Shoe Talk: Writing Imaginary Conversations for Shoes

TO THE TEACHER/PARENT: ABOUT THE LESSON

This lesson is comprised of only an introduction and a series of prompts for eliciting imaginary conversations among shoes. So this is an exercise in basic personification, not the kind encountered in poems and novels.

EVALUATING STUDENT RESPONSES

About the only thing you can evaluate in this lesson is the use of quotation marks. That is, all of the "conversations" between the various shoes should be enclosed by quotation marks. Otherwise, the responses of your students are a matter of their imagination and ingenuity. They can come up with any number of ideas for the shoe talk, and theirs may be considerably different—and probably better—than ours. Following are the quips that we attributed to the various shoes. Some are old song titles.

1. "Do I smell something?"
2. "I've got a crush on you."
3. "Ouch!"
4. "Do you have to be so airy?"
5. "Don't be so hard on me."
6. "What makes you so nervous?"
7. "You're all wet!"
8. "Softly, as in a morning's sunrise."
9. "I get a kick out of you!"
10. "Hi, Brownie."
11. "In a few years, you'll be looking more like me."
12. "You're a square from nowhere."
13. "That sure is a pointed remark."
14. "We're both well-heeled."
15. "Are you always so tipsy?"
16. "Ha! You can't get the lead out!"
17. "What are you—Hopalong Cassidy?"
18. "Hi, Flattie."
19. "Why don't you grow up?"
20. "Waltz me around again, Willie."

Targeted Learner Outcomes: The student will

- use quotation marks to enclose the conversation of the shoes, and
- compose conversations for a variety of shoes.

Name: _____ Date: _____

Lesson 10: Personification

Shoe Talk

A. Shoes are important. We are reminded of this constantly by the shoe companies. How can Americans wear so many shoes? There are shoes for kicking, running, walking, climbing, jumping, dancing, golfing, lounging, gardening, and even swim-

ming. They are springy, hard, soft, square, air-cushioned, flexible, and holey. Shoes can be worn, bronzed, taped, colored, laced, unlaced, and discarded.

If shoes could talk, what would they say? What would a baseball player's shoe and a golfer's shoe say to one another? Would it be "Hi, Spike."?

Directions: Think of what various shoes might say to each other in greeting. Be sure to enclose their conversations with quotation marks.

1. What would a ballroom dancer's shoe say to a gardener's shoe?

   _____

2. What would a football player's shoe say to a ballerina's slipper?

   _____

3. What would be the ballerina slipper's reply?

   _____

4. What would a wooden shoe say to a sandal?

   _____

5. What would the sandal say in reply?

   _____

6. What would a runner's shoe say to a tap dancer's shoe?

   _____

7. What would a workman's boot say to a swimmer's light, tight shoe?

   _____

8. What would a pair of moccasins say to each other?

   _____

Name: _____ Date: _____

Lesson 10: Personification

Shoe Talk (cont.)

9. What would a soccer player's shoe say to the soccer ball?

_____

10. What would a yellow shoe say to a brown shoe?

_____

11. How would the brown shoe reply to the yellow shoe?

_____

12. What would a pointed-toe shoe say to a square-toed shoe?

_____

13. What would the square-toed shoe reply?

_____

14. What would a cowboy's boot say to a financier's dress shoe?

_____

15. What would a wedge-shaped shoe say to a high-heeled shoe?

_____

16. What would a tennis player's shoe say to a deep-sea diver's shoe?

_____

17. How would the deep-sea diver's shoe reply?

_____

18. What would a basketball player's shoe say to a policeman's shoe (but not a policewoman's shoe)?

_____

19. What would a high rubber boot say to a galosh?

_____

20. What do the dancer's shoes say to each other between dances?

_____

Lesson 11: Analogies

Whales: Making Analogies; Writing a Cinquain

TO THE TEACHER/PARENT: ABOUT THE LESSON

An effective way to teach the writing of cinquains to a class is to begin by having the students do some analogizing. This is the methodology of "Whales." Your students are first to consider how whales and teenagers can be compared. Next, they are to compare seven pairs of living things. Then they are to compose a cinquain. The analogizing will get them in the mood to think about the characteristics of their subjects, and the cinquain can then be quickly composed.

EVALUATING STUDENT RESPONSES

If the lesson comes off well, you should have no trouble in encouraging your students to write additional cinquains. Since they are so brief, cinquains usually don't take long to compose. The pattern presented in the lesson of 1-2-3-4-1 words is simpler than the one that has 2-4-6-8-2 syllables and is generally easier for young people to follow. Don't worry too much if some of the lines are too long or too short. Students have written very successful cinquains that didn't conform exactly to the pattern.

Targeted Learner Outcomes: The student will

• make seven analogies about living organisms, and

• write a cinquain about one of them.

Name: _____ Date: _____

Lesson 11: Analogies

Whales

A. When most people see teenagers, they aren't reminded of whales, but there are some similarities.

- Young people are like whales whose rapid growth poses difficult problems at times.

- Young people are whales that must emerge regularly from their element to view a sometimes hostile world.

- Young people are whales in the sea of knowledge, filtering and digesting bits of information at an incredible rate.

- Like whales, young people can be trained to be very clever and to perform tricks for audiences.

- Young people are whales whose blowing off steam is more indicative of natural processes than of a bad nature.

Comparisons such as these are called **analogies. An analogy points out a similarity in things that are otherwise unlike.** In the extended analogy above, teenagers who ordinarily aren't compared with whales are found to have some traits in common with the huge animals.

Directions: In like manner, can you point out similarities between the items in each of these pairs?

1. a penguin and a frog _____

_____

2. a pugilist and a dentist _____

_____

3. a moth and a sunflower _____

_____

4. a librarian and a squirrel _____

_____

Lesson 11: Analogies

Whales (cont.)

5.   an anteater and a woodpecker _____

_____

6.   a seagull and a jackal _____

_____

7.   a tap dancer and a rooster _____

_____

B. Select one of your analogies and think more deeply about the two things. For example, the analogy of the teen and the whale could inspire a cinquain such as this:

Whales
Big eaters
Blowing off steam
But underneath hurting, caring
Teens

Cinquains have five lines, and one kind of cinquain has a pattern of 1-2-3-4-1 words for those lines.

First line—One word, giving the subject
Second line—Two words about the subject
Third line—Three words, expressing action
Fourth line—Four words, expressing feeling
Fifth line—Another word for the subject

Directions: Try writing a cinquain about one of your analogies in the space below.

_____

_____

_____

_____

_____

Lesson 12: Irony

You Don't Mean It: Composing an Ironic Limerick

TO THE TEACHER/PARENT: ABOUT THE LESSON

One professor we knew stated that sarcasm is "irony without understanding." We like that definition, but in practice, irony and sarcasm are sometimes indistinguishable. Generally speaking, however, sarcasm is harsher and often expressed without genuine humor.

Limericks are a lot of fun to compose because the rhythm of the five lines is not difficult to imitate and the purpose of all limericks is to provide humor. The rhyme scheme is AABBA, and the rhythm is a rough anapestic of 3, 3, 2, 2, and 3 feet. The example in the lesson of a critic's complaint about having to *hear* a play follows the pattern of a limerick exactly.

For most students, catching on to the form and rhythm of a limerick is easy. Perhaps those who do not follow the pattern so easily can be put on track by repeatedly listening to limericks that conform. Edward Lear's famous limericks can be recited or passed out to the class.

Your students may or may not readily think of ironic themes for their limericks. It is possible that you will have to give cues to the ones who struggle to come up with an idea. These are ironies that could be developed into limericks: winning/losing, loving/hating, saving/spending, falsity/truth, appearance/reality.

Targeted Learner Outcomes: The student will

• gain an understanding of what constitutes an irony, and

• write a limerick containing an irony.

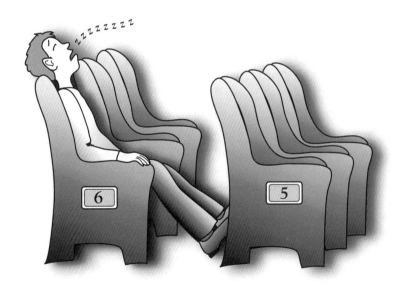

Name: _____ Date: _____

Lesson 12: Irony

You Don't Mean It

A. If you are sensitive to them, life presents many ironies every day. An irony occurs when a combination of circumstances results in the opposite of what might be expected. **Irony in speaking and writing is a device used to deliberately express ideas so that they can be understood in two ways.**

These are some memorable ironic statements:

- Mark Twain was supposed to have said something like: "It's no trick to give up smoking—I've done it dozens of times."

- "I married beneath me. All women do." That statement was made by Nancy Astor.

- "I never forget a face, but in your case I'll make an exception" was uttered by Groucho Marx.

- An advertisement for Marvelous Marv's Auto Repair: "I'll treat your car better than I treat my own."

- Aldous Huxley said: "Armaments, universal debt, and planned obsolescence—those are the three pillars of Western prosperity."

B. This is a famous limerick that expresses the flavor of irony very well:

> Bob Benchly, fatigued at a play,
> Protested, while slipping away;
> "They've ruined the spell
> By *pronouncing* too well.
> You can hear every word that they say."

Directions: See if you can work some irony into a limerick. As you know, a limerick has five lines. The first, second, and fifth lines rhyme with each other, and the third and fourth lines rhyme.

_____

_____

_____

_____

_____

Lesson 13: Hyperbole

Three in a Row: Writing a Humorous Narrative Featuring Hyperbole

TO THE TEACHER/PARENT: ABOUT THE LESSON

It may well be that hyperbole is the most common figure of speech in your students' speech. They just naturally say things in exaggerated ways. In fact, this lesson may come as a mild shock to them because they probably have never considered expressions such as "I could have slept for a year" and "That book weighs a ton" as being figurative ways of speaking.

You might take the opportunity to point out that "most perfect" in the first example given of an exaggerated statement is also grammatically wrong, as is the popular "very unique." Once something can be considered as perfect, its perfection can't increase. Similarly, "unique" means "one of a kind"—if it is one of a kind, it doesn't need the intensive "very."

The writing assignment is a tricky business, mostly because writing humor is so difficult to do well. However, for inexperienced writers, the tendency in writing humor is actually to exaggerate, and so they will employ hyperbole rather naturally. The trouble lies in their using it too broadly.

Targeted Learner Outcomes: The student will

- learn the definition of hyperbole, and

- write a humorous narrative that features hyperbole.

Lesson 13: Hyperbole

Three in a Row

A. Hyperbole, or exaggeration, is a figure of speech used to emphasize a statement or situation. It is a common device, though usually unconscious, of young people in putting over their ideas. Words such as always, perfect, forever, and never are often used in these exaggerations. These statements all feature hyperbole.

- That was the most perfect party anyone has ever given.

- I was so starved I ate everything in sight!

- She walks so slow it's like she's going backwards.

- There were more people at that concert than I've ever seen in one place before.

- No lawyers can really be trusted.

B. Hyperbole is often used to emphasize a point, an opinion, or a situation. In some cases, it serves as a way of creating humor. The following piece is an example of the latter purpose, although it may not have been intentional.

It always happens that way. I mean, she can never let it go. If I mention something like ice cream or dessert, Leah starts telling that story about when she went to Crider's with that guy. What's his name now … oh yeah, Purvis. Funny name, isn't it? Anyway, Purvis invites her to Crider's for ice cream or something, and Leah sits there, all proud because Purvis is one special hunk.

It goes pretty well for Leah at first. She orders some low-fat ice cream dish, and Purvis orders a banana split. You know, one of those humongous banana splits they serve. When he manages to get through his banana split—Leah eats her little dish of ice cream as slowly as she can so as to appear dainty-like and not too famished—this dreamboat orders another banana split! Leah's mouth falls open. And here it comes—another humongous banana split. He eats that just as nonchalantly as the first one.

Leah is making as if to get up from the table when Purvis says casually, "Those sure were good. I think I'll have another." Leah is now dying of embarrassment. And people are starting to stare. You know how they always stare anyway when the server brings in those huge banana splits. Leah's face is getting redder and redder, but Purvis isn't noticing.

When he gets halfway through the third banana split, Leah excuses herself and goes to the ladies' room. When she returns to the table, she gets a shock. There is Purvis with his head on the table. He's passed out! She has one dickens of a time reviving him so he can pay the check. Leah always ends up the story by saying, "Darned if I was going to pay to see that guy make a hog of himself!" That was their last date.

37

Name: _____ Date: _____

Lesson 13: Hyperbole

Three in a Row (cont.)

Directions: See if you can write three or four paragraphs that use hyperbole to inject humor into a little story. The story can be taken from one of your experiences, or it can be fictional. **Narrative paragraphs are made up principally of the details of a series of happenings that are given in chronological order.** Generalizations and comments are used sparingly. It is the sequence of events that comprises the body of the narrative and that builds up interest in the reader.

_____

_____

_____

_____

_____

_____

_____

_____

_____

_____

_____

_____

_____

_____

_____

_____

_____

_____

_____

_____

_____

Lesson 14: Hyperbole

Tall Tales: Writing a Tall Tale

TO THE TEACHER/PARENT: ABOUT THE LESSON

This lesson invites students to exaggerate. The exercise is intended to simply get your students to write. The ideas they come up with then may be turned into tall tales.

It may be that none of the dozen sentences that they have transformed into hyperbolic prose will spark an idea for a tall tale. If so, allow your students to take off on any idea that they can find to get their imaginations going.

EVALUATING STUDENT RESPONSES

The biggest temptation that many of your students will have in writing their tall tales will be going too far in their exaggerations. It will probably be a good idea to have them pair off and read their tales to one another after they have written their first drafts. Before you do that, however, gently tell them that even with this kind of storytelling, there must be limits, and they shouldn't strain credibility too much.

Targeted Learner Outcomes: The student will

- convert 12 sentences into examples of hyperbole, and

- write a tall tale.

Lesson 14: Hyperbole

Tall Tales

A. These are the kinds of statements that can be typically found in American folklore.

- That ship carried over six hundred men, and some of those men never saw all of their shipmates on a two-year voyage.

- The words that he would rather shoot a sheriff any day than rob a bank was known so well that sheriffs invariably locked themselves in and barred the doors or left town when "Pretty Boy" was in the area.

- Hawley stated that the air was so pure in that place that people never died, unless by accident.

- Our hero reached the interesting age of 250 years and was in perfect enjoyment of his health and every faculty of mind.

- The hogs were so exceedingly kind and accommodating to Maine emigrants as to approach their barnyards once a week to be butchered.

- After the long dust storm, one man opened the door of his car and found ground squirrels overhead tunneling upwards for air.

Americans have always enjoyed exaggerated tales of daring, strength, and cunning. Paul Bunyan, Mike Fink, John Henry, Joe Magerac, and Davy Crockett are just a few of the characters that have been featured in these tall tales. **A tall tale is a greatly exaggerated story told mostly for the humor in it.** Although it is said that everyone exaggerates at some time, very few people ever exaggerate to the extent that the chroniclers of the deeds of Paul Bunyan, Pecos Bill, and Stormalong have done.

B. Just for fun, make these straightforward sentences into exaggerated statements.

1. Gorham made the majority of his team's tackles from his linebacker's position.

   _____

   _____

2. Tina was considered a good pilot. _____

   _____

Name: _____ Date: _____

Lesson 14: Hyperbole

Tall Tales (cont.)

3. The traffic was slow. _____

_____

4. Frank found himself amongst a bunch of daredevils. _____

_____

5. A sudden gust of wind knocked the little craft about on the sea. _____

_____

_____

6. The family was rich. _____

_____

7. His generosity was well known. _____

_____

8. The hot sun made the travelers uncomfortable. _____

_____

9. Ants occasionally invade the house. _____

_____

10. An odd sound came up from the cellar. _____

_____

_____

11. Many people mourned the death of the popular entertainer. _____

_____

_____

12. Pintar was a master of disguises. _____

_____

C. Take one of those dozen sentences that you have blown up into exaggerations as the idea upon which to base a tall tale. Your tall tale won't be like those in American folklore; it will be a modern tall tale. Make it as colorful as you can. Write the tall tale on your own paper.

Lesson 15: Sayings

Epigrams Are Witty: Translating an Epigram Into a Verse

TO THE TEACHER/PARENT: ABOUT THE LESSON

The title of the lesson almost says it all. Epigrams are hard to distinguish from other sayings, but they can always be identified by their humor. Therefore, epigrams are enjoyable. They are also brief, as are maxims, aphorisms, and proverbs.

The task for the student engaged in this lesson is to convert an epigram into a short verse. We mention the couplet and quatrain, but your students can choose any kind of verse. Although we present them with ten witty sayings, they do not have to choose from among those. Your students may have trouble composing their verses, however, and so you should allow enough time for them to develop their ideas.

EVALUATING STUDENT RESPONSES

The two requirements of selecting a genuine epigram and of translating it into a verse are your major concerns in evaluating the individual students in this lesson. Since there is considerable emphasis upon the witty nature of epigrams in this lesson, we don't anticipate that your students will go wrong there (besides, we have given them a dozen examples of the epigram), but they may find it challenging to write a successful verse that puts over the epigram's essence.

Targeted Learner Outcomes: The student will

- become aware of the nature of an epigram, and

- translate an epigram into a verse.

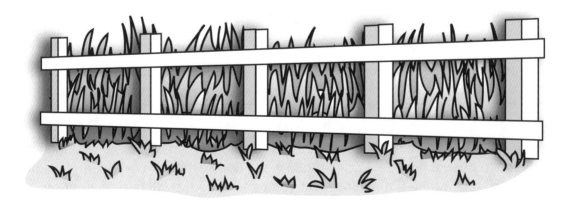

Name: _____ Date: _____

Lesson 15: Sayings

Epigrams Are Witty

A. According to one encyclopedia, **"An epigram is a short, witty poem or pointed saying."** Originally, epigrams were in verse. The definition of an epigram, in fact, is covered in this famous couplet:

> What is an epigram? A dwarfish whole,
> Its body brevity, and wit its soul.

> —Samuel Taylor Coleridge

B. Nowadays, epigrams are generally found in prose, but they aren't as common as they once were. You might find it amusing to put an epigram in the form of a verse, taking a well-known one in prose and converting it into a verse. Like Coleridge's verse above, you might make it a couplet, or you might put it into an *ABAB* rhyme scheme as a quatrain. For example, the epigram "Experience is what everyone calls his mistakes" can be made into a four-line verse in this way:

> Although we err in the most obvious way
> And blunder ever so often,
> It's only "experience," we say,
> And our goofs we thereby soften.

You can translate any epigram into a short verse of two or four lines, or you can use one of the following as your inspiration.

- The grass is always greener on the other side, but it's just as hard to mow.

- It's no disgrace to be poor, but it might as well be.

- If it looks like a duck, walks like a duck, and quacks like a duck, it is a duck.

- It pays to pester.

- Some people get paid for giving advice while others think they should give it away free.

- Kindness is loving people more than they deserve.

- Chop your own wood—it will warm you twice.

- Never interrupt when you are being flattered.

- You do not have to keep running after you have caught the bus.

Name: _____ Date: _____

Lesson 15: Sayings

Epigrams Are Witty (cont.)

Directions: Write the first drafts of your verses in the space below. You will probably want to translate more than one epigram into verse in order to see which one turns out best.

_____

_____

_____

_____

_____

_____

_____

_____

_____

_____

_____

_____

_____

_____

_____

_____

_____

_____

Lesson 16: Sayings

Fabulous Sayings: Writing Fables Based on Proverbs

TO THE TEACHER/PARENT: ABOUT THE LESSON

The first part of the lesson about proverbs is meant to set up the writing activity of producing an original fable. For those students quite familiar with fables, the task should not be difficult. It isn't certain, however, that all of your students read or had told to them the fables of Aesop or LaFontaine when they were younger. Possibly some may have read the modern fables of Lionni, Steig, Alexander, Ciardi, Titus, and Daugherty.

The fables that the students create can be quite short. Paraphrasing the proverb first may give them ideas for their little stories. Since they are asked to find additional proverbs, this lesson is one for which time should be allotted to go to the library or to take the lesson home.

Targeted Learner Outcomes: The student will

- find five suitable proverbs and list them, and

- write an original fable based on a proverb.

References:

Alexander, L. *The Four Donkeys.* New York: Holt, Rinehart and Winston, 1972.

Ciardi, J.J. *Plenty and Fiddler.* Philadelphia: Lippincott, 1963.

Daugherty, J. *Andy and the Lion.* New York: Viking, 1938.

Kent, J. *Fables of Aesop.* New York: Pantheon, 1973.

Lionni, L. *Frederick.* New York: Pantheon, 1967.

Lionni, L. *Fish Is Fish.* New York: Pantheon, 1970.

Scarry. R. *The Fables of LaFontaine.* Garden City: Doubleday, 1963.

Steig, W. *Amos and Boris.* New York: Farrar, Strauss, 1971.

Titus, E. *Anatole and the Cat.* New York: McGraw-Hill, 1957.

Name: _____ Date: _____

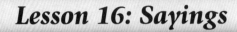

Lesson 16: Sayings

Fabulous Sayings

A. A proverb is a short saying in common use that strikingly expresses some obvious truth or familiar experience. The language is usually picturesque and simple. Only those sayings that many people have used for a long time are called proverbs. Whereas maxims are usually pieces of advice ("Don't burn the candle at both ends."), proverbs are given in the form of a statement. They point out virtues and vices, such as cooperation, greed, gullibility, timidity, cunning, self-reliance, faithfulness, unselfishness, and patience.

These are familiar proverbs:

- Many hands make light work.

- When it rains, it pours.

- Still waters run deep.

- It's hard for an empty sack to stand upright.

- Alcohol and gasoline don't mix.

- A bird in the hand is worth two in the bush.

- Marry in haste; repent at leisure.

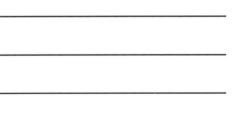

B. Look in reference books or on the Internet and find at least five additional proverbs that appeal to you.

1. _____

2. _____

3. _____

4. _____

5. _____

Name: _____ Date: _____

Lesson 16: Sayings

Fabulous Sayings (cont.)

C. A fable is a short tale that teaches a lesson or moral. The characters in a fable are usually animals who act like human beings, but sometimes they are people. Each character stands for something good (like being kind or wise) or something bad (like being greedy or vain). Some of the most familiar fables we have were created by Aesop, a Greek slave who lived 2,600 years ago. The one about the fox and the grapes is one of his most famous.

A hungry fox once saw some fine luscious grapes hanging temptingly from a vine above his head. He leaped and snapped and leaped again, but he could never quite reach the grapes. So many times did he try that he tired himself out completely, and it was some time before he could drag himself limping away, angry with the world and with himself. As he went along, he grumbled savagely to himself, "What sour things those grapes are! No gentleman would want to eat them."

To make sure the reader gets the point, a moral is placed at the end of the fable. For the fable of the fox and the grapes, this was added by Aesop: "Every man tries to convince himself that the thing he cannot have is of no value." James Thurber wrote some modern fables, such as "The Little Girl and the Wolf." The moral for this "Fable of Our Time" is: "It is not so easy to fool little girls nowadays as it used to be."

D. Select a proverb that you can use as the basis for a fable. You can use the proverb just as it is, as the moral of the fable, or you can reword it. For example, "A stitch in time saves nine" could be paraphrased: "A little forethought will prevent a lot of grief." After looking at many proverbs, write the one you will use for your fable here. Write the fable on your own paper.

_____

_____

_____

_____

_____

Lesson 17: Paradox

Internal Strife: Putting Paradoxes Into Advertisements

TO THE TEACHER/PARENT: ABOUT THE LESSON

A true paradox is a puzzle; you ask yourself, "What does it really mean?" The contradiction must put some doubt in a person's mind for there to be a paradox. Because it is powerful, paradox is a valuable tool for writers, but it must be used so that it doesn't confuse or frustrate the reader. The trouble is that writers who use paradoxes enjoy the contradictory situations, but their perceptions sometimes make their readers uncomfortable.

Before you and your students tackle "Internal Strife," we should issue a warning: it is one of the most difficult lessons in this book. For example, if your students were to be asked to compose a paradoxical statement for Rodney's Record Retreat, a store featuring used records and discs, one of them might come up with "Music for hungry ears and skinny purses." That slogan is clever, but it is not a paradox. There is no contradiction inherent between "hungry ears" and "skinny purses." If the student keeps thinking hard at coming up with a contradiction, he or she might think of "If the tune is catchy, we've caught it," but that is merely a pun. So, you see, this lesson is challenging.

EVALUATING STUDENT RESPONSES

These are some attempts at devising paradoxical slogans for the seven products and services. They are mostly our attempts, but two were actually found in ads in the yellow pages.

1. A-1 AUTO WRECKING "Where the parts are greater than the wholes."
2. THE ELYSIAN SPA (specializing in mud baths) "The dirtier you get, the cleaner you become."
3. ROMELLI'S BAIL BONDS "You're out before you're in."
4. SOLEM'S MATTRESSES "Inexpensive … not cheap."
5. DENNY'S ELECTRIC (specializing in compressors) "A little compressor that is *very big*."
6. FOSTER REALTY "Your property is our property."
7. PAUL'S PARACHUTES "Double your money back if proved unsatisfactory."

Targeted Learner Outcomes: The student will

- understand what a paradox is,

- explain four paradoxical statements, and

- devise paradoxical statements for seven products and services.

Name: _____   Date: _____

Lesson 17: Paradox

Internal Strife

A. There are many paradoxical situations in life, and writers love to point them out. **A paradoxical statement has elements that seem to contradict each other.** Following are a few paradoxes that have amused and sometimes puzzled people. Explain each one.

1. The Detroit community is more than sixty percent minority. _____

_____

_____

2. In growing older, we become more foolish—and wise. _____

_____

_____

3. When you add to the truth, you subtract from it. _____

_____

_____

4. We have to believe in free will—we have no choice. _____

_____

_____

5. It's easier to cheat a very smart person than it is to cheat a very dumb one. _____

_____

_____

Name: _____ Date: _____

Lesson 17: Paradox

Internal Strife (cont.)

B. A famous advertisement about luggage proclaimed: "The real beauty of it isn't the beauty of it." That might well mean that the appearance of the luggage wasn't its greatest asset. Undoubtedly the person who wrote the ad had a good sense of humor. A bank advertised: "We're the same—only we're better." It would seem that some advertising copywriters like to use paradoxical statements to catch the reader's eye. Using a paradoxical statement to enliven prose or poetry or to capture the attention of readers requires some thinking.

Directions: See if you can write paradoxical statements to be used in ads for these products and services.

1. A-1 AUTO WRECKING _____

   _____

2. THE ELYSIAN SPA (specializing in mud baths) _____

   _____

3. ROMELLI BAIL BONDS _____

   _____

4. SOLEM'S MATTRESSES _____

   _____

5. DENNY'S ELECTRIC (specializing in compressors) _____

   _____

6. FOSTER REALTY _____

   _____

7. PAUL'S PARACHUTES _____

   _____

Lesson 18: Oxymorons

The Successful Failure: Explaining Oxymorons

TO THE TEACHER/PARENT: ABOUT THE LESSON

Inasmuch as the oxymoron seems to be losing none of its popularity, your students should consider it as a literary device to be used occasionally in their writings. It shouldn't be used too often, of course, and it should only be used when the writer wants to make a point or to get the right effect.

The oxymorons presented in the lesson are of varying degrees of difficulty. Your students may have no trouble explaining a "devilish angel," for example, but they could be stumped with "soothingly upsetting" or "openly stealthy." Encourage them to keep thinking if an explanation does not occur right away.

EVALUATING STUDENT RESPONSES

These are possible explanations for the 12 oxymorons. Many others can be offered that are just as satisfactory.

1. successful failure—There are several ways to interpret this phrase. An individual who sets out to fail and does so is a successful failure. (This does happen.) Another individual who is considered a failure by some criterion (money is the usual one) can be successful in other ways (such as being a loving person).

2. devilish angel—We see quite a few devilish angels among young children. They are angels in looks but devils in deportment.

3. gloomy clown—Some clowns have gloomy faces painted on, and many clowns are reputed to be privately melancholy. There's a theory that all comedians are essentially unhappy people.

4. painful pleasure—An example of this could be long-distance runners who experience a "high" but also a good amount of pain.

5. popular outcast—There have been a number of political exiles who were very popular with the people and who came back to lead them.

6. virtuous sinner—This oxymoron suggests the hypocrite who wants to appear virtuous but who is really sinful in his behavior. Literature abounds with this type.

Lesson 18: Oxymorons

The Successful Failure: Explaining Oxymorons (cont.)

7. healthy invalid—A person can be confined to a wheelchair because of the loss of a limb but be otherwise quite healthy.

8. an ancient youth—We occasionally see men and women who are trying to look and act young but who are obviously considerably past their prime.

9. soothingly upsetting—Individuals who try to console others at the wrong times can be upsetting.

10. cheerfully mournful—Some people attend funerals and seem to be fairly cheerful about it. (Which we feel, incidentally, is okay.)

11. mournfully cheerful—It is true that someone can act in a mournful way—by kidding—in order to cheer others up. The mournfulness would have to be exaggerated.

12. openly stealthy—Someone can deliberately act in a stealthy way in order to attract attention to himself for some reason.

13. aggressively shy—Some people seem to insist upon being regarded as shy and retiring.

14. tactfully discourteous—It is possible to be discourteous at the "right times" (when you want to be discourteous and when it doesn't create a commotion or hurt people you don't want to hurt).

15. a correct mistake—Occasionally, we make a mistake, and it turns out that it was the right thing to do after all.

16. enforced freedom—To be free is not to be coerced, but there have been times when an individual didn't want to be free, as when a convict wished to stay in prison for some reason.

Targeted Learner Outcome: The student will supply explanations for 12 oxymorons.

52

Name: _____ Date: _____

Lesson 18: Oxymorons

The Successful Failure

A. In recent years, the well-named device called **oxymoron,** which means "sharp/dull" in Greek, has become immensely popular. Writers use it especially in titles for films, books, songs, articles, and advertisements. As its name indicates, **the elements of an oxymoron are contradictory.** Nevertheless, the oxymoron is meant to convey an idea that is feasible, one from which the listener or reader can readily get some meaning.

James Thurber, a keen student of the English language, offered this example of a double oxymoron: "That building is a little bit big and pretty ugly." Actually, if anyone were to make that exact comment aloud, very few people would fail to get its meaning.

In a different vein, a writer has given us *Back to the Future* as a title. How can we go back to the future? Apparently, everyone knows because this expression is so often used that it is almost trite.

B. Following are a dozen oxymorons that are intended to make some kind of sense. Explain how they make sense to you.

1. successful failure _____

   _____

2. devilish angel _____

   _____

3. gloomy clown _____

   _____

4. painful pleasure _____

   _____

5. popular outcast _____

   _____

6. virtuous sinner _____

   _____

Name: _____ Date: _____

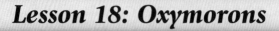

Lesson 18: Oxymorons

The Successful Failure (cont.)

7. healthy invalid _____

_____

8. an ancient youth _____

_____

9. soothingly upsetting _____

_____

10. cheerfully mournful _____

_____

11. mournfully cheerful _____

_____

12. openly stealthy _____

_____

13. aggressively shy _____

_____

14. tactfully discourteous _____

_____

15. a correct mistake _____

_____

16. enforced freedom _____

_____

Lesson 19: Oxymorons

Squaring the Circle: Explaining Oxymorons; Writing a Short Story

TO THE TEACHER/PARENT: ABOUT THE LESSON

Since oxymorons have become so popular, there will probably be no need to dwell on the definition of this fascinating figure of speech. Your students should mentally take the term in stride. Explaining how "flat but bumpy" might make sense, however, could cause your students to think. Accordingly, provide enough time for them to work on the dozen prompts.

EVALUATING STUDENT RESPONSES

The following are among a host of interpretations that can be made of the 12 oxymorons.

1. flat but bumpy—There can be roads that traverse a flat terrain but have potholes in them and are therefore bumpy.

2. weak but strong—Some people appear to be weak in body, but they are strong-minded.

3. a kindly villain—There have been many villains who have performed acts of kindness even though they were acting in illegal or oppressive ways. To the Sheriff of Nottingham, Robin Hood was a villain.

4. a stupid genius—Many brilliant people are stupid about everyday things such as figuring out how to program a VCR or how to balance a checkbook.

5. a familiar stranger—A person who you've never met before but who reminds you of someone is a familiar stranger.

6. a blank picture—Amazingly, there have been framed "pictures" with nothing on the canvas ("a field of snow on a bleak day," for example). They were probably hoaxes.

7. a squared circle—By definition, circles can't be square, of course; but a circle can be encompassed by a square, thus producing a squared circle, and this is not uncommon in designs.

8. a genuine phony—This is an absolute phony—a veritable phony.

9. a worthless treasure—Children often find "fool's gold" and believe they have come upon a treasure, but the value of the rocks is virtually nil (except in their eyes).

Lesson 19: Oxymorons

Squaring the Circle: Explaining Oxymorons; Writing a Short Story (cont.)

10. a dry shower—The shower could be of leaves or dust.

11. gracefully clumsy—Although a few people move in a clumsy way, they manage to be graceful about it and don't stumble, fall, or bump into things.

12. childishly mature—Some individuals attempt to act in a very grown-up manner, but their intentions are so obvious that they are actually rather childish.

In evaluating your students' short stories, you might give them some tips about the elements that make the stories interesting to readers. They can aim to give their stories humor, vividness, original settings or plots, unusual twists in style or content, and original endings. To heighten interest, their stories should have a personal touch and naturalness, show the feelings of the characters, and have variety in the length and structure of the sentences.

Targeted Learner Outcomes: The student will

• explain 12 oxymorons, and

• write a short story.

Name: _____   Date: _____

Lesson 19: Oxymorons

Squaring the Circle

A. Occasionally people say or write things that seem to contradict them-selves. For example, someone might remark about a "warm winter" or "going nowhere." (How can anyone be going if he doesn't get any-where?) Here are some expressions that have parts that don't seem to agree with each other. Perhaps you can make sense of them. In the space given, explain what each phrase might mean.

1. flat but bumpy _____

    _____

2. weak but strong _____

    _____

3. a kindly villain _____

    _____

4. a stupid genius _____

    _____

5. a familiar stranger _____

    _____

6. a blank picture _____

    _____

7. a squared circle _____

    _____

8. a genuine phony _____

    _____

9. a worthless treasure _____

    _____

Name: _____ Date: _____

Lesson 19: Oxymorons

Squaring the Circle (cont.)

10. a dry shower _____

_____

11. gracefully clumsy _____

_____

12. childishly mature _____

_____

Expressions such as "a genuine phony" and "a familiar stranger" are called **oxymorons. An oxymoron is a figure of speech in which opposite or contradictory ideas or terms are combined.**

B. Can you think of any other expressions that, at first glance, seem to be self-contradictory? If you can, explain how they might really be sensible after all.

Expression   **Interpretation**

_____   _____

_____   _____

_____   _____

_____   _____

_____   _____

See if any of your classmates can figure out some good explanations for your contradictory expressions.

C. Why don't you take one of your expressions or one of the other contradictory expressions and write a short story about it? First, think about the characters that would be in your story, where they might be, what they would be doing, and when the events would take place.

Name: _____ Date: _____

Lesson 19: Oxymorons

Squaring the Circle (cont.)

Next, write the story line, or plot, in the space below. Finally, on your own paper, rewrite your story, taking out parts that don't fit and putting in descriptions, conversations, or facts that will make the story richer and more enjoyable to read. Be sure to proofread your story for errors in punctuation, spelling, and usage so that others can fully appreciate what you are writing about, but don't worry about any mistakes until you have written out your story completely.

_____

_____

_____

_____

_____

_____

_____

_____

_____

_____

_____

_____

_____

_____

_____

_____

_____

Lesson 20: Neologisms

New Words: Inventing and Translating Made-Up Words

TO THE TEACHER/PARENT: ABOUT THE LESSON

Although most of us have made up a word or two, either intentionally or unintentionally, it was probably in our younger days. Therefore, this lesson will likely appeal more to your students than it does to you. It's essentially light-hearted, but its basis is the serious matter that words are added to the English language constantly. New scientific words derive largely from Latin, but other everyday words are often coined by writers. Some words derive specifically from the people who are responsible for the idea, for example, *bowdlerize* from Thomas Bowdler, who expurgated Shakespeare, and *spoonerisms* from W.A. Spooner, who transposed words hilariously. Then there are words that come from stories and plays, such as *malapropism* after Mrs. Malaprop in Richard Sheridan's *The Rivals.*

EVALUATING STUDENT RESPONSES

Actually, this is a challenging lesson. Your students are to translate words such as "fribby" and "elesiary" as well as to coin a dozen words of their own. The following are acceptable translations of the neologisms in the story about the student daydreaming.

elesiary = fanciful, light, airy, etc.

fribby = easy

sacol = private

zorf = young, pretty, difficult, crazy, lovable, etc.

mekko = zombie, airhead, ding-a-ling, etc.

Targeted Learner Outcomes: The student will

- translate five made-up words in a story, and

- coin a dozen original words for regular ones.

Lesson 20: Neologisms

New Words

A. When you were very young, did you ever make up words? Little children, when they are learning to speak, often make up words that are close to legitimate words. Later on, you may have coined some new words for the private use of you and your close friends.

Scientists regularly make up words for newly discovered animals and plants and heavenly bodies. Names must be coined for new drugs and new products too. So our language is constantly acquiring new words. From time to time, because they need words that don't exist, writers coin words, and many of these words have been adopted into the language. **New words are called neologisms.**

B. Translate the underlined words in this little story. Write what you think the words mean above each underlined word in the selection.

DAYDREAMER

Maria spent her after-school hours from 4:00 until 6:00 that day on homework, but she

was only there in body, not in spirit. Her <u>elesiary</u> mind was working on math problems, more or

less, which had always been really <u>fribby</u> for her. Not much thinking was required, and it never

interfered with her <u>sacol</u> dreams, when in spirit she

traveled to exotic foreign lands with her <u>zorf</u> friend

Alexis. In her mind's eye they are catching a plane

and flying off to romantic places. The strange sites

and smells of those new places seem so real to her,

that if her fellow students could see her now in her

trance-like state, they would think she was kind of

a <u>mekko</u>. I think it just proves that Maria has a vivid

imagination!

Name: _____ Date: _____

Lesson 20: Neologisms

New Words (cont.)

C. Can you come up with new words for the following?

1. twinge (n.) _____

2. knit (v.) _____

3. berry (n.) _____

4. plod (v.) _____

5. paper (n.) _____

6. tool (n.) _____

7. antique (n.) _____

8. pebble (n.) _____

9. button (n.) _____

10. agree (v.) _____

11. gasp (v.) _____

12. fuzzy (adj.) _____

13. lightning (n.) _____

14. computer (n.) _____

15. a new cough drop that doesn't have codeine or sugar

    _____

16. a newly discovered satellite of Jupiter

    _____

THE ALL NEW NEW WORD DICTIONARY

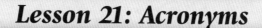

Lesson 21: Acronyms

Abbreviations: Deciphering Acronyms

TO THE TEACHER/PARENT: ABOUT THE LESSON

Although there have been acronyms in American speech and writing for a very long time, they have never been so popular as they are now. Young people use acronyms, of course, and so the device will be quite familiar to your students. One or two of the acronyms to be deciphered may be somewhat hard to figure out, but all of the ten are in everyday use throughout the country.

EVALUATING STUDENT RESPONSES

The ten acronyms that are to be deciphered are as follows:

1. SWAT = special weapons and tactics

2. DOT = Department of Transportation

3. PAT = point after touchdown

4. IRA = individual retirement account;
    Irish Republican Army

5. COLA = cost of living allowance

6. SAT = Scholastic Assessment Tests

7. ERA = earned run average; Equal Rights Amendment

8. AIDS = acquired immune deficiency syndrome

9. FDIC = Federal Deposit Insurance Corporation

10. NASCAR = National Association for Stock Car Auto Racing

Targeted Learner Outcomes: The student will

•   decipher ten common acronyms, and

•   list 15 additional acronyms that are used today.

Name: _____ Date: _____

Lesson 21: Acronyms

Abbreviations

A. In an effort to save time or space, we often use acronyms in our speech and in our writing. **An acronym is a word formed by the initial letters of a name or by combining initial letters or parts of words.** The habit of using acronyms instead of the words they stand for has become more pronounced in recent years. Rarely does anyone say "Internal Revenue Service," especially in March or April. We say "IRS." The origin of some acronyms is actually unknown to the great majority of people, as in the cases of *radar* for <u>ra</u>dio <u>d</u>etecting <u>a</u>nd <u>r</u>anging and *Fiat* for the Italian car <u>F</u>abbricato <u>I</u>talia <u>A</u>utomobilia <u>T</u>orina.

    The practice in writing is to use the words that the acronym stands for at the beginning of a discussion and then to use only the acronym afterward. Sometimes, if the acronym is not familiar, a reader has to go back to the beginning to read what it stands for in order to understand what the acronym means.

B. What do these acronyms stand for? If you don't know offhand, you can look them up.

1. SWAT _____

2. DOT _____

3. PAT _____

4. IRA _____

5. COLA _____

6. SAT _____

7. ERA _____

8. AIDS _____

9. FDIC _____

10. NASCAR _____

Name: _____ Date: _____

Lesson 21: Acronyms

Abbreviations (cont.)

C. Find at least 15 additional acronyms that are used by people regularly. Write the acronyms and their definitions below.

1. _____

2. _____

3. _____

4. _____

5. _____

6. _____

7. _____

8. _____

9. _____

10. _____

11. _____

12. _____

    _____

13. _____

    _____

14. _____

    _____

15. _____

    _____

Lesson 22: Onomatopoeia

Fizz, Gurgle, and Burp: Coining Words That Imitate Sounds

TO THE TEACHER/PARENT: ABOUT THE LESSON

Dictionaries identify words that imitate sounds as "echoic." The fancier term is onomatopoeia; but if a dictionary says "origin probably echoic," the word is one of a great many in English that are highly useful. These words are approximations of the sounds that we hear, and they can be used effectively in some kinds of writing.

In this lesson, your students are asked to invent words that imitate a variety of common sounds. If they can imagine the sounds, they can probably manage to approximate them in letters. In cases where students are unable to hear the sounds in their minds, you might allow them to do some experimenting outside the classroom.

Targeted Learner Outcomes: The student will

- name the sights evoked by 15 onomatopoetic words, and

- create appropriate words in imitation of 15 sounds.

FOLLOWING THROUGH

- Have your students spend 15 minutes at home or at school listening for familiar sounds that aren't usually described by onomatopoetic words, such as the scraping of metal upon metal.

- Have your students take any three onomatopoetic words and put them in a sequence that will suggest a scenario or little story. They can then illustrate their stories.

- Find three or more songs such as "Pop Goes the Weasel" that contain onomatopoetic words.

- Ask them what the dictionary designation is for onomatopoetic words. ("echoic")

- You might also have your students invent words for specific sounds, for example, sounds made by machines, insects, and pets. Have them think of a sound in each of those three categories that doesn't already have an onomatopoetic word associated with it. Be sure that they check in a dictionary to make sure their words are original.

Name: _____ Date: _____

Lesson 22: Onomatopoeia

Fizz, Gurgle, and Burp

A. When human beings first started to speak, they must have found certain common sounds useful as words. These were the sounds themselves—words such as *buzz, chirp, pop,* and *glug.* Words such as those and *whiff, fizz, gurgle,* and *hiss* imitate natural sounds. The name given to this kind of word is **onomatopoeia.**

Directions: What do you visualize when you hear these words?

1. click _____

2. gurgle _____

3. glug _____

4. clank _____

5. beep _____

6. twang _____

7. rat-a-tat _____

8. swish _____

9. twitter _____

10. hiss _____

11. thwack _____

12. oomph _____

13. thump _____

14. clang _____

15. squish _____

67

Name: _____ Date: _____

Lesson 22: Onomatopoeia

Fizz, Gurgle, and Burp (cont.)

B. It is quite likely that most of the words for sounds in section A will remain in the English language indefinitely. However, there are probably quite a few common sounds that do not as yet have words applied to them. Can you come up with words that imitate these sounds? Write your new word on the line next to each sound description. Check in the dictionary to make sure you are not using a word that already exists.

1. the sound of a small waterfall _____

2. the sound of a toaster as it pops up a piece of bread (It isn't *pop*.) _____

3. the sound of a pencil writing fast on a piece of paper _____

4. the sound of a match being struck _____

5. the sound of a referee's whistle at a ballgame (It's not really *tweet*.) _____

6. the sound of the shuffling of a deck of cards _____

7. the sound of a chair scraping when it is being pushed back on a hardwood floor

   _____

8. the sound of the sudden inhaling of breath _____

9. the sound of skidding tires on wet pavement _____

10. the sound of rustling leaves in the autumn _____

11. the sound of air escaping from a balloon _____

12. the sound of a suppressed sneeze _____

13. the sound of wind coming through a crack between a window and its casement (*Whistling* is the usual word.) _____

14. the sound of fingernails scraping on a chalkboard

    _____

15. the sound of a stifled yawn

    _____

Lesson 23: Sentence Sense and Review

Subjects and Predicates: Identifying Subjects and Predicates; Recognizing Literary Devices

TO THE TEACHER/PARENT: ABOUT THE LESSON

This lesson is concerned with two things, namely, sentence sense and a review of the literary devices featured in this book. Except for the sentences that have the understood subject "you," the sentences are not difficult to analyze. A presumption is made that your students have had previous grammar lessons about what constitutes a subject and a predicate, and so those terms are not defined.

EVALUATING STUDENT RESPONSES

Your students are to identify as many of the various literary devices as represented by the 15 sentences as they can. Since a few can be identified in more than one way, there may be some debate as to the correct answers. You shouldn't make too much of your students' scores, although this lesson is a good way for you to know whether or not your students have really understood the devices that have been presented in this book.

These are our answers.

1. Benton bought books for the needy boys.   Alliteration
2. The search for happiness is one of the chief sources of unhappiness.   Paradox
3. Look before you leap. The subject is the understood "You."   Maxim
4. A little inaccuracy sometimes saves tons of explanation.   Epigram
5. The devil popped up like a grinning jumping jack.   Simile
6. Don't learn traffic laws by accident. The subject is the understood "You."   Pun
7. The moon gently kissed the summit of the hills.   Personification
8. Take the bull by the horns and do it! The subject is the understood "You."   Metaphor
9. In the same way that a fisherman lets out still more line in landing a game fish, the con man gave the elderly woman one promise after another.   Analogy
10. She torgled a lot that summer.   Neologism
11. He was so tall he couldn't tell when his feet were cold.   Hyperbole
12. Mrs. Anthony is tired of the hurly-burly of modern living.   Rhyme (Hinky-Pinky)
13. There are not ten writers in Boston equal to Shakespeare.   Irony
14. Larry is a cheerful pessimist.   Oxymoron
15. The threat of being exposed seized his heart with an icy grip.   Metaphor, Personification

Targeted Learner Outcomes: The student will
* identify the subject and predicate of 15 sentences, and
* designate the type of literary device exemplified by each sentence.

Name: _____ Date: _____

Lesson 23: Sentence Sense and Review

Subjects and Predicates

A. Writers sometimes have fragments of sentences serve as sentences because there is no need to fill in all of the words of a thought. To put it in the form of a paradox, the fragment is complete, although it is incomplete. An example is:

> Once she knew she had you in her power, she'd never let go—not for an instant. Terrible woman!

It wasn't necessary for the author to write "She was a terrible woman!" because those words are understood. On the other hand, inexperienced or careless writers write incomplete sentences unknowingly. A careless student might write a sentence such as this and be quite unaware that it isn't correct and may be confusing to a reader:

> Pictured above in front of her house on the river, a quick glimpse of living as Sally imagined it to have been like a hundred years ago.

The first part that is missing is the all-important subject of the sentence. Who is pictured in front of the house?

A fundamental way of finding out if you have or haven't written a complete sentence is to see if you have both a subject and a predicate.

B. Following are 15 sentences. Underline the subjects of these sentences once and their predicates twice. Then go back and identify what kind of literary device is used in each sentence. Write the name of the literary device on the line at the end of each sentence.

1. Benton bought books for the needy boys. _____

2. The search for happiness is one of the chief sources of unhappiness. _____

3. Look before you leap. _____

4. A little inaccuracy sometimes saves tons of explanation. _____

5. The devil popped up like a grinning jumping jack. _____

6. Don't learn traffic laws by accident. _____

7. The moon gently kissed the summit of the hills. _____

Name: _____ Date: _____

Lesson 23: Sentence Sense and Review

Subjects and Predicates (cont.)

8. Take the bull by the horns and do it! _____

9. In the same way that a fisherman lets out still more line in landing a game fish, the

    con man gave the elderly woman one promise after another. _____

10. She torgled a lot that summer. _____

11. He was so tall he couldn't tell when his feet were cold. _____

12. Mrs. Anthony is tired of the hurly-burly of modern living. _____

13. There are not ten writers in Boston equal to Shakespeare. _____

14. Larry is a cheerful pessimist. _____

15. The threat of being exposed seized his heart with an icy grip. _____

Lesson 24: Persuasive Essays

Summer Vacation: Analyzing a Persuasive Essay

TO THE TEACHER/PARENT: ABOUT THE LESSON

You should present "Summer Vacation" to your students before administering "Who's to Blame?" because it will give them a chance to examine a persuasive essay written by someone closer in age to them than almost any of the essays that they will read. Accordingly, the essay has its deficiencies insofar as being a model to imitate, although it epitomizes the main feature of the genre—that is, it is written entirely from a personal perspective. We hope that by seeing how it could be improved that your students will be made aware of some of the crucial elements in a persuasive essay.

EVALUATING STUDENT RESPONSES

It seems to us that the student's essay can be analyzed and assessed thusly:

1. The writer relied mostly upon personal anecdotes to make her argument that young people should do something worthwhile with their time during summer vacation. She provided quite a few details about her experiences at the camp, and some of them can definitely be classified as facts. This essay is written strictly from a personal viewpoint, and so her experiences and attitude about doing something rewarding are quite legitimate.

2. The thesis statement doesn't come until the beginning of the last paragraph: "So if you would like to work hard for low pay, but enjoy something very rewarding during your summer vacation, Camp Callahan is the place to be."

3. Yes, she defines "Camp Callahan."

4. Yes, a number of facts (mostly about camp procedures and equipment) are provided.

5. Answers will vary.

6. The writer didn't spend much time giving a counter-view about spending time during summer vacation (for instance, working to save money or just relaxing).

In a way, it would be hard to improve upon this essay as one written from a purely personal viewpoint. The writer's audience is her fellow students. However, students who do not have a sympathetic nature or would like to earn more money during the summer will probably not be persuaded to work at such a camp.

Targeted Learner Outcome: The student will critique a persuasive essay about summer vacation.

Name: _____ Date: _____

Lesson 24: Persuasive Essays

Summer Vacation

A. Following is a persuasive essay written by a student in high school. Read it once fairly quickly, and then read it again so you can answer the following questions.

1. What among the following is the main technique used by the writer in putting across her argument?

   facts   **examples**   **anecdotes**
   quotes by authorities   **comparisons**   **analyses**
   rebuttal of contrary opinions

   _____

   _____

2. Is there a thesis statement? If so, what is it? _____

   _____

3. Did the writer define any of the terms she was using? Is so, which ones? _____

   _____

4. Did she provide any facts in her essay? If so, name a few. _____

   _____

   _____

5. Was her argument convincing to you? Explain. _____

   _____

   _____

6. How could the essay be improved? _____

   _____

   _____

Name: _____ Date: _____

Lesson 24: Persuasive Essays

Summer Vacation (cont.)

"LOW PAY, VERY REWARDING"

Ah, summer. The time when school is empty and students do anything they want for three months. Well … some students. I know people who have done nothing this summer; I know people who have worked all summer and made some pretty good money; and then there's me. After high school, I'm thinking about a career in special education, so I answered an ad for a Camp Callahan counselor. The ad began "Low pay, very rewarding." For those of you who don't know, Camp Callahan is a camp for the physically and/or mentally handicapped. For one week out of the year, the campers are allowed to feel just like everyone else. No one stands out from the others or gets stared at because they're "different." The slogan was "Yes I can at Camp Callahan." No matter the disability, every camper has the option to do every activity. Even those in wheelchairs have the opportunity to go on "walks," and to go horseback riding and swimming.

The counselors are employed for four weeks. The camp runs from Sunday evening to Friday afternoon for each group of campers. Your time off consists of Friday evening until Sunday afternoon and one, six-hour period during the week. Some of your shifts consist of all-nighters to periodically check on the campers. There is no fee for the camper, and since the camp is run entirely on donations, the pay is minimal. I'm not going to say it's not hard work because it is. However, the joy you experience when you hear a woman with crippled legs laugh while you're pushing her wheelchair down a trail because she is "running" is something I wouldn't trade for any high-paying job.

The first week is your training for the weeks to come. You learn to pitch tents and do chores as well as supervise the campers, who are referred to as "buddies." The second week is for the most severely handicapped. Each camper, because of his or her extreme disabilities, has his or her own counselor for personal super-

74

Lesson 24: Persuasive Essays

Summer Vacation (cont.)

vision. That is the most difficult week for most of the counselors. It is very physically and emotionally difficult. Many of the campers can't speak and/or can't walk and have several different disabilities. You soon learn to understand your camper's hand gestures or odd speech. You help him go to the bathroom, get dressed, take him on "walks," help him eat meals, and make his life something very special for that one week where he can be "normal." The third week is for handicapped adults. The fourth week is for handicapped kids. During these weeks, since the campers are more self-sufficient, each counselor has two to three campers each.

Every Sunday night when the campers arrive, we have a fishing contest. During the week, we have cookouts, do skits, arts and crafts, and sing songs. At the end of the week is the big dance. Everyone gets all dressed up, and it is a very exciting event for all. The deejay of the music machine sets up flashing lights, a disco ball, and plays music. To transport everyone for all outdoor activities, we use a huge yellow truck that pulls a wagon for those in wheelchairs. It has a ramp and benches. All of the campers love traveling on the truck because we go on bumpy roads. The only way to coax one man off the wagon was to sing him a country-western song and promise him catsup on his food! One time a police officer came to camp and turned on his lights and sirens. The kids' faces with their looks of wonder were something to see after they experienced something that most people take for granted. Amy, one of my little campers, would only wear dresses and patent leather shoes to camp. She would cry if you wanted her to wear shorts and sensible shoes. So during arts & crafts, I made her a fairy wand to go with her pretty dress, and she played with it all week. My reward was the huge smile on her face on receiving something that was simply made from paper and glitter. Kyle, another camper, loved to swim so much that once he was in, he'd refuse to get out of the water, so we'd have to carry him out.

So if you would like to work hard for low pay but enjoy something very rewarding during your summer vacation, Camp Callahan is the place to be. It's made me stop and enjoy the simple things in life that I never noticed before.

Lesson 25: Persuasive Essays

Who's to Blame?: Writing a Persuasive Essay

TO THE TEACHER/PARENT: ABOUT THE LESSON

"Who's to Blame?" is a serious lesson that is meant to get your students thinking about critical issues and then to lead them into an essay-writing activity. The lesson contains no levity, but it can involve students emotionally. In fact, the essay writing won't be successful unless the students feel strongly about the problems that are presented. You may want to add one or more problems that you believe would be provocative for your students.

EVALUATING STUDENT RESPONSES

You might want to duplicate the following checklist for your students to consult while they are writing their essays after they have finished their first drafts. It also can be presented on a chalkboard or as a transparency on an overhead projector.

Checklist After First Draft

When you have finished your essay, you should ask yourself a few questions.

1. Did I make a thesis statement at the beginning?

2. Do I have facts, examples, and/or anecdotes to support my opinion? The evidence given is the most important part of the essay.

3. Did I avoid the use of broad generalizations instead of presenting facts? Generalizations of widely accepted ideas are more effective than generalizations that rest upon vague assumptions.

4. Did I organize my facts, examples, and anecdotes in such a way as to present a persuasive argument?

5. Did I demonstrate that I had a clear idea of what I wanted to say?

6. Did I make an emphatic restatement of my argument at the end of the essay?

It works out well for students to pair up after writing their first drafts in order to discover inconsistencies, errors, and lack of organization in their essays.

Targeted Learner Outcomes: The student will

- consider some serious problems confronting us and name "culprits" responsible for the problems,

- write a persuasive essay about one of the problems, and

- use a checklist to ensure that he or she has put up an effective argument.

76

Name: _____ Date: _____

Lesson 25: Persuasive Essays

Who's to Blame?

A. It's hard for us to admit our mistakes. It's just as hard to admit our faults. Politicians seem to have that problem more than most of us. When asked why something went wrong, they seem to always have an explanation, but often it stretches the limits of credulity to the breaking point. Coaches, managers, and fans have the same tendency in the world of sports. They sometimes say they have won or lost because one side was obviously better or worse than the other, but such frankness is relatively rare.

Directions: Who would you like to blame—and make it stick—for these problems? Pick the person, organization, group, institution, natural phenomenon, or country that you would receive the greatest pleasure in blaming. You don't have to pick the one that is really most responsible, but do so if you wish.

Problem	Culprit
moral decline	_____
overpopulation	_____
extinction of endangered species of plants and animals	_____
terrorism	_____
bad streets	_____
huge national debt	_____
corrupt politicians	_____
rising divorce rate	_____
crime	_____
drunk driving accidents	_____
illiteracy	_____

Name: _____ Date: _____

Lesson 25: Persuasive Essays

Who's to Blame? (cont.)

B. Select a problem about which you feel most strongly and formulate a statement about it. What should be done?

_____

_____

_____

C. Write a persuasive essay that gives your views and also makes a proposal to do something about the problem. An essay has a thesis statement (which you have written above) and presents an argument that is backed up with facts, comparisons, examples, quotations by authorities, anecdotes, and analyses. You don't have to have all of these elements in your essay, but you should have some of them in it in order to convince readers of your position. Consider what the audience for your essay will be. Will it be for the general public, for young people of your age, or for a special group of people? You will want to do some research for your essay by consulting reference books, the Internet, and authorities.

It is a good idea to make an outline of the major points of your essay before you begin your first draft. Use the space below for your outline.

_____

_____

_____

_____

_____

_____

_____